WAITING FOR GOD

tragicomedy in one act

A PLAY by
VI KHI NAO

The Rectangular Repertory production of *Waiting for God*
was first presented by Samuel Beckett at the
Mark Taper Forum in Las Vegas, Nevada, on
March 6, 2036. The cast was:

        Eliquis   Apichatpong Weerasethakul
        Abigatra   Elizabeth Bishop
        Ngủ   Hồ Xuân Hương
        Kohlrabi   Kristina Tonteri

The play was directed by Lucky Estragon Vladimir

Set design by Ming Cho Lee
Costume design Eiko Ishioka
Lighting design by Zeus
Music by The Weeknd
Augment direction by David Fincher
Dramaturg for the production was Philip Seymour Hoffman
The Production Stage Manager was Ali Raz

This production played at the 890 Theatre in New York City,
Produced by the Rectangular Repertory Company for seven years
Starting May 18, 2036; and at the Royal Georgia Theatre
in Chicago, produced by the Steppenpanther Theatre Company,
beginning on September 10, 2036

Waiting for God opened in New York City at the Plyteeth Theatre on
October 16, 2036, produced by Ben DeVos, Roberto Bolaño,
Lady Gaga, Meryl Streep, Edward Norton, Anthony Bourdain,
Trịnh Xuân Thanh, Mỹ Huyền, and Steve Jobs

Waiting for God was written on commission from God
& the Rectangular Repertory Company

CHARACTERS:

Eliquis

Abigatra

Ngủ

Kohlrabi

WAITING FOR GOD

Copyright © 2022 by Vi Khi Nao

No part of this book may be reproduced in any form by any electronic or mechanical means including photocopying, recording, or information storage and retrieval without permission in writing from the author.

ISBN-13: 978-1-954899-63-6
ISBN-10: 1-954899-63-7

Cover artwork: 'Covetousness' by Sara Baun
Cover design by Matthew Revert

www.apocalypse-party.com

First Edition

Printed in the U.S.A

WAITING FOR GOD

ACT I

6th dimension of time. An x-ray machine.

Morning.

ELIQUIS, *standing near the x-ray machine, is attempting to wear a lead x-ray apron. She tries to lift it with her fingers, sighing.*

She releases it, it falls. She is weak, composes herself, lifts the apron up and is confounded by its weight.

Enter ABIGATRA.

ELIQUIS:
 (*exasperated*). Somebody has to give in.
ABIGATRA:
 (*drawing closer to an established, congruent reality of place, aka nowhere*). It has the shape of infinity. It was just yesterday that everything was easier. (*asserting*). Be soft and gentle,

not everything has to be inside a loop. So I tried not baking for once. (*She ruminates, making faces with her fingers. Eye-rolling towards* ELIQUIS.) So what is going on with you?

ELIQUIS:

What?

ABIGATRA:

I thought you were somebody else. I'm pretty certain that you're a blood thinner.

ELIQUIS:

I am!

ABIGATRA:

But you're NOT, I reassure you! I have to find out. Will it be costly? (*She thinks to herself.*) May I pour you a glass of whiskey first?

ELIQUIS:

(*happily*). Not if you want to lose your leg.

ABIGATRA:

(*unhappily, defiantly*). Try not to bite my head off, but where did you wait for God?

ELIQUIS:

Inside an x-ray machine.

ABIGATRA:

(*sympathetically*). Really? Without wearing an apron?

ELIQUIS:

(*eyebrows raised*). That machine.

ABIGATRA:

And cancer didn't become your lover?

ELIQUIS:

How should I know? Radiation walks home alone quietly. At night.

ABIGATRA:

Not only at night.

ELIQUIS:

In the morning. In the afternoon. Quite a way from here. So what?

ABIGATRA:

It seems impossible . . . decades of possibility . . . but each layman . . . how time folds itself . . . (*Resolutely*.) You and I are subatomic particles, sitting and waiting and being dead like electromagnetic waves, but waving to nobody translucent.

ELIQUIS:

How translucent are we talking here?

ABIGATRA:

(*disconsolately*). Not ghostly, I mean. Humanly as possible. Certainly not dead (*Silence. Jauntily*). Well, for one thing, it has to be detected before being measured. And God is impossible. We should take all kinds of therapy we are allowed. What choices do we have?

ELIQUIS:

It can't be that hard to find someone translucent and decent.

ABIGATRA:

Wilhelm Röntgen. Where is this German physicist now? On December 22, 1895, he x-rayed his wife's hand! The first man to do so. While she wore her wedding ring. Did he invent radiology or was it his way of exploring her infidelity potential? (ELIQUIS *plays with her shirt's buttons.*) Are you anxious?

WAITING FOR GOD

ELIQUIS:
> Removing my shirt so I can be half-naked. Have you been naked before?

ABIGATRA:
> I fear my shirt is getting in the way of putting on that lead apron. It is obvious, isn't it? Are you blind or are you being impossible?

ELIQUIS:
> (*insipidly*). Forgive me!

ABIGATRA:
> What is with you?

ELIQUIS:
> (*frantically*). Life! She aches for my impartiality!

ABIGATRA:
> (*indignantly*). How could she ache for it when she *is* unfairness, the definition of inequity? What have you got to say for yourself?

ELIQUIS:
> Can't you ache for something you can't have?

ABIGATRA:
> (*miserably*). Don't defend her. Defend me.

ELIQUIS:
> (*directly*). You are not a hypocrite.

ABIGATRA:
> Spot on. (*She adjusts her bra straps.*) Balance is so important.

ELIQUIS:
> You always let your bra tilt you down the wrong path.

ABIGATRA:
> (*ponderingly*). That's impossible . . . (*She ponders.*) I always

straighten it out whenever I can so that one side is not too crooked.

ELIQUIS:

Lend me a hand with this apron, will you?

ABIGATRA:

The world seems seconds away from collapsing. Later it holds itself together. (*She takes off her bra, plays with its cups, shouts into them like they are megaphones, rubs them against her face, drops them on the ground.*) I am done with you! . . . Am I? (*She contemplates its mortality.*) . . . certainly. (*Without weight*). Uncertain. (*She lifts the bra off the ground, inspects the parameters of the cups.*) How witty. (*She taps on the center of the cup as if to send a message to it via Morse code, flips it over, drops it down to the ground.*) It's ignoring me. (ELIQUIS *has removed her shirt. She lets it hang in the air by the tips of her fingers, allows it to swing back and forth like a windchime, drops it on the floor, picks it up, studies the texture of its fabric and engineering condition, places one of the cups against her ear, listens to it intently.*) So?

ELIQUIS:

Are you listening in?

ABIGATRA:

Or is it speaking to me?

ELIQUIS:

Well?

ABIGATRA:

I can't hear a thing.

ELIQUIS:

(*probing her left breast*). Shall I let them hang a bit?

WAITING FOR GOD

ABIGATRA:
> If you are waiting for God, that isn't the way you go about it. (*She drops the bra on the ground, twirls it awkwardly with her shoes, then jumps on it, picks it up, presses it against her ear, listens.*) This headphone is WAY too big for us. (*Stillness. ABIGATRA, lost in translation. ELIQUIS stretches her nipple.*) It must have been designed by one of God's archangels. (*Beat.*) God shouldn't outsource critical works. (*Beat.*) No go.

ELIQUIS:
> You can't blame him for your inability to listen.

ABIGATRA:
> What if we cry?

ELIQUIS:
> Because the bras aren't behaving like microphones or headphones?

ABIGATRA:
> Right . . . (*She mumbles.*) But tear ducts can abduct.

ELIQUIS:
> God's interest? Sympathy?
> ABIGATRA *sneezes, covers her hand over her nose. Her nose wiggles.*

ABIGATRA:
> Only the nose can do so.

ELIQUIS:
> Frightful adversity.

ABIGATRA:
> It all exists in the hate. (*She tries to mimic the facial composition of hatred.*)

Hating the nose and not the tear ducts. Absolutely this. (*Beat.*) I forgive you.

ELIQUIS:

(*crossly*). I hate Vietnamese postmodern poetry. I can't stand it.

ABIGATRA:

That came out of nowhere. You find it that repulsive?

ELIQUIS:

Of course . . . (*She echoes.*) It's worse than witnessing a hyena speaking French.

ABIGATRA:

Do you remember Satan?

ELIQUIS:

Hmmm, that omnimalevolent figure who has chosen God to be his adversary? He is an ambitious one. Maybe more psychological than psychotic. He's handsome, that one? I couldn't be sure. The Dead Sea would probably know. Is he the one that makes me hungry during my menses? I've used this shofar on the Prince of Darkness and I'll tell you nothing baffles or complicates him. I'd like to swim with him.

ABIGATRA:

You sound like an idiot.

ELIQUIS:

An idiot would sound smarter than me. (*She focuses on the x-ray machine.*) Now tell me about the apple of discord for idiocy!

ABIGATRA:

What?

ELIQUIS:
>Tell me!

ABIGATRA:
>Of course, an idiot is smarter than an imbecile, but an imbecile is dumber than a retard and a retard—

ELIQUIS:
>Is more of an idiot than a stupid person.

ABIGATRA:
>No.

ELIQUIS:
>I really don't know the hierarchical order of a moron.

ABIGATRA:
>Let me give you a model of *your* imbecility. The most decent example of a pinhead is the Jobs.

ELIQUIS:
>Steve Jobs? The business magnate.

ABIGATRA:
>No no. God's Job.

ELIQUIS:
>God was employed by whom?

ABIGATRA:
>(*crossly*). What the hell? God was employed by God, idiot.

ELIQUIS:
>Of course, God had Job. That's why he didn't need a job!

ABIGATRA:
>God doesn't need to be hired... (*Beat.*) ... by ANYONE — what I want to say, clearly, is that Satan is so marvelous. God was bragging to Satan, more like taunting him.

Job is the model denizen of virtue—the most obedient, upright man—and Satan impishly refutes God by telling him that the reason prosperous Job is so virtuous is because God protects him (*Beat.*) And, to bait God, Satan tells him that the reason why Job is good and not being blasphemous towards God is because God has been kind to him.

ELIQUIS:

So what did he do?

ABIGATRA:

In order to win the spat and to show Satan that he was right, God proceeds to take, without Job's permission, of course, everything from Job. His wife was gang-raped and murdered by the Junko Furuta rapists, all of his children died of leukemia, and he lost all of his wealth when he invested in Ethereum.

ELIQUIS:

(*with extravagant fervor*). What was Job thinking?

ABIGATRA:

What was God thinking? He allowed his dominance to get to his head. That's why.

ELIQUIS:

Poor God.

ABIGATRA:

NO, poor Job's wife and children.

ELIQUIS:

I mean—

ABIGATRA:

Can you imagine your lives were taken away just to

prove a point? Also, while he suffers like no one suffers, Job didn't say a mean thing to or about God.

ELIQUIS:

True. True.

ABIGATRA:

What I am trying to say is, if God is all omnipresent, omnipotent, why does he need to unethically duel with an ape like Satan? Satan is completely out of his league. It is like—

ELIQUIS:

Cristiano Ronaldo competing against Lionel Messi.

ABIGATRA:

No, cretin. It's like Muhammed Ali thumping Peter Buckley.

ELIQUIS:

Who is Peter Buckley?

ABIGATRA:

My point.

ELIQUIS:

So did God win or not?

ABIGATRA:

God lost because he won.

ELIQUIS:

What kind of winning is that?

ABIGATRA:

The kind that one shouldn't repeat. I mean, what if genocide, say the Holocaust, happens because of a degenerate duel between one superomnipotent being and one alleged, semi-superomnipotent figure—say

God against Satan—Satan says to God, "I bet Judaism will cease being an active religion if you kill off 6 million of its followers."

ELIQUIS:

And, God replied, "Watch me?"

ABIGATRA:

Something like that. Before the evening gets away from us—

ELIQUIS:

I just want to say that Steve Jobs isn't like Job at all. In the end, he has all of that wealth, but then he died of pancreatic cancer.

ABIGATRA:

What if the opposite of evil is wanting things as they are? Not wealthier, not more beautiful daughters? Not a second exquisite wife after being forced into widowhood?

ELIQUIS:

Meaning what, that wanting things to stay the same is a sign of goodness?

ABIGATRA:

Exactly. I think—

ELIQUIS:

I think Jobs's wife, Laurene, has really beautiful eyes. I think they are blue. Blue like the sky after Noah's ark docked on the edge of the earth after a massive rainstorm. *(She moves arduously, cupping her left breast, stops, examines the x-ray machines with her shoulder, presses her body against the center of the machine, turns around to lean against it.*

ABIGATRA *observes her, then walks to the bra on the floor, shouts into the cups, and exhales.*)

ABIGATRA:
Brown! But who cares. I think the Job parable truly informs us that Satan and God switched roles. (*She spits into one of the bra's cups.* ELIQUIS *drifts away from the machine, faces the audience.*)

ELIQUIS:
God becomes Satan by allowing Satan to bait him. (*She turns her back to the audience.*) Stimulating projection. (*She waves to* ABIGATRA.) Turn that on!

ABIGATRA:
I won't do it.

ELIQUIS:
How come?

ABIGATRA:
I'm waiting for God.

ELIQUIS:
(*desolately*). So… (*Suspense*). That God can defend himself?

ABIGATRA:
No.

ELIQUIS:
Who asked us to wait?

ABIGATRA:
The x-ray machine.

ELIQUIS:
The x-ray machine says that?

ABIGATRA:
Look at the ticker on top. It clearly says, "Wait—

ELIQUIS:
>(*reads with her*). For God.

ABIGATRA:
>It can't be.

ELIQUIS:
>Do you think it's broken?

ABIGATRA:
>Out of the question.

ELIQUIS:
>Is that even an x-ray apparatus?

ABIGATRA:
>A time machine.

ELIQUIS:
>A Moses shrub pretending to be—

ABIGATRA:
>William Roentgen. Does time exist inside of us or outside of us?

ELIQUIS:
>What do you mean?

ABIGATRA:
>I mean that time machine—does it work by us being near it? Or—

ELIQUIS:
>Do we have to be inside?

ABIGATRA:
>There are no doors to the inside of an x-ray machine. Can't you see? What's wrong with you?

ELIQUIS:
>What about two days from now?

WAITING FOR GOD

ABIGATRA:
>Never, imbecile!

ELIQUIS:
>Couldn't they invent one?

ABIGATRA:
>What I'm trying to say is—

ELIQUIS:
>The machine is heartless. Can't even reinvent itself from an x-ray into a time machine.

ABIGATRA:
>Utterly ruthless.

ELIQUIS:
>Won't even come with a door that we could enter.

ABIGATRA:
>Ah, of course, this is where you are sinful.

ELIQUIS:
>How sinful?

ABIGATRA:
>Erroneously sinful. Altering the nature of time also alters the content and composition of the object.

ELIQUIS:
>Thus, time changes everything. Including time itself and the objects surrounding it.

ABIGATRA:
>No! (*Wrathfully*). Perhaps you are right, the x-ray machine at some point in his unfluctuating state of chemical imbalance, due to his excessive exposure to photons, most likely, decides it's best for him to alter his gender, I mean, to alter his physical entity to match the content of his psychological and emotional soul.

ELIQUIS:

So basically, an x-ray machine has a sex(ual) operation—

ABIGATRA:

(*eyeing around*). That is downright nonsexual, by becoming a time machine.

ELIQUIS:

Do you think God would approve?

ABIGATRA:

Of the operation?

ELIQUIS:

No, dummy! An x-ray machine doesn't need the approval of God for anything!

ABIGATRA:

Well . . . what . . . (*rotating towards the audience*). then…?

ELIQUIS:

Would God be okay if the x-ray machine became a better version of himself, a.k.a GOD?

ABIGATRA:

Time is not another dimension of God. And, even if time is God, time isn't better than God.

ELIQUIS:

We're yakking about the time machine, here. (*Silence.*) Right? And, not time.

ABIGATRA:

No.

ELIQUIS:

No what?

ABIGATRA:

We're talking about sex reassignment surgery, I think.

ELIQUIS:
>Of the x-ray machine.

ABIGATRA:
>In which the object being operated on is also simultaneously a surgeon.

ELIQUIS:
>How is it possible that the surgeon is the patient?

ABIGATRA:
>Just ask time. (*She gropes the exterior pockets of her jeans, searching.*)

ELIQUIS:
>(*very curiously*). What are you searching for?

ABIGATRA:
>I am (*Silence.*) Probing? (*Silence.*) For a watch.

ELIQUIS:
>A watch can tell?

ABIGATRA:
>Well, if the time machine is the surgeon and the x-ray machine is the patient and the transformation couldn't have happened without a time machine, the surgeon, then it makes sense that (*gazing riotously about her, as if the ticker of her thoughts is scrolled across the clouds*) the surgeon is the patient. So so so… it's imaginable!

ELIQUIS:
>A watch didn't tell us that. You just did.

ABIGATRA:
>A watch is somewhere on me.

ELIQUIS:
>You want me to believe that since it is near you it has

chosen your body, your mouth, precisely, to voice its thought?

ABIGATRA:

No no...

ELIQUIS:

Well... (*Silence.*) What is it then?

ABIGATRA:

(*frailly*). I was about to ask time if it knows anything about its mother. (ELIQUIS *leans against the x-ray machine. ABIGATRA leaps restlessly up and down, landing briefly every second to observe the machine. ELIQUIS falls into a trance. ABIGATRA sits down next to* ELIQUIS.) ELIQ! . . . Eliq! . . . ELIQ! (ELIQUIS *blinks her eyes, startled.*)

ELIQUIS:

(*reinstated to the terror of* ABIGATRA's *logic*). But an x-ray machine doesn't give birth to time! (*Wretchedly*). Why won't you believe me?

ABIGATRA:

What does it give birth to?

ELIQUIS:

Images. It uses photons to create images.

ABIGATRA:

Get out!

ELIQUIS:

I kid you not—

ABIGATRA:

But when an x-ray becomes a time machine, what does this time machine give birth to?

ELIQUIS:

(*motion towards the cosmos*). Infinite versions of realities.

(*Beat.*) It's so impolite of you to force me to state the obvious, Gatra. Through your mindless inquiries, you can turn a sane person insane. A sightseeing person blind.

ABIGATRA:

I only ask because I want clarity.

ELIQUIS:

(*frostily*). Clarity of what?

ABIGATRA:

Do you think this time machine has memories of her former x-rayed self?

ELIQUIS:

How should I know? (*Silence.*) Does it, Gatra, matter? (*Silence.*) Does it matter what you ate yesterday or the day before? (*Silence.*) What good does it to reflect on irreversibility? (*Silence.*) Does it, Gatra?

ABIGATRA:

Compose yourself.

ELIQUIS:

(*obesely*). Compose . . . com-post . . . From Latin.... *composita*.... (*Silence.*) Feminine and neuter.

ABIGATRA:

Speaking of recycled organic material, if you have memories of what you were once before, wouldn't you use that memory in service of your most recent life?

ELIQUIS:

No.

ABIGATRA:

Say...take photographs of the various versions of yourself while transforming into a time machine?

ELIQUIS:

If you were an ex-x-ray machine, you would do that?

ABIGATRA:

NEVER!

Exit ABIGATRA swiftly. ELIQUIS stands up and trails her as far as the boundary of the page. Signals and contortions of ELIQUIS are similar to a vulture attacking a rat. Enter ABIGATRA. She walks by ELIQUIS, traverses the page of the script with eyes closed. ELIQUIS folds her body like a piece of paper.

ELIQUIS:

(*softly*). Why not? (*Silence. ELIQUIS unfolds herself and makes four strides backward.*) Why are you taking this so personally? (*Silence. One foot backward.*) Gatra . . .

ABIGATRA:

(*rotating*). Don't let me be lonely.

ELIQUIS:

(*falls backward*). Are you okay? (*Silence. Recollects herself*). I don't mean to be insensitive. (*Silence. Retreats a little. ELIQUIS extends her arms from afar, giving ABIGATRA an airhug from a distance.*) Please, Gatra. (*Silence.*)
ELIQUIS *flinches*.
You hugged me too tight!

ABIGATRA:

I got carried away. (*Silence. ELIQUIS studies civilly at the machine.*) You think God forgot us?

ELIQUIS:

No.

WAITING FOR GOD

ABIGATRA:

How do you know?

ELIQUIS:

He said wait for him.

ABIGATRA:

It says 'Wait for God'—it could have been commanded by anyone.

ELIQUIS:

(*vastly animated*). By the machine!

ABIGATRA:

Maybe. If it was written by God, shouldn't it say 'Wait for me?'

ELIQUIS:

Me could be anybody.

ABIGATRA:

If you were God you would be so fucked. (*They walk towards and lean their bodies against the machine.*) God couldn't even leave a voicemail on anyone's phone that says, "Hello, it's me… I was wondering if after all these years you'd like to…"

ELIQUIS:

He tried.

ABIGATRA:

That's why he addressed himself in the third person singular?

ELIQUIS:

Using that fat pre-x-ray time machine turned smartphone?

ABIGATRA:

Possibly.

ELIQUIS:

Why don't you run that machine on me?

ABIGATRA:

What for?

ELIQUIS:

Maybe that's how God talks to us, imbecile!

ABIGATRA:

What if the machine time travels you?

ELIQUIS:

Where would I go? Use your intuition will ya?

ABIGATRA *applies her sixth sense.*

ABIGATRA:

(*conclusively*). I have nothing

ELIQUIS:

Let's just wait for him (*She insinuates.*) Maybe . . . maybe . . . (*Calmly*). God will bring a tablet, his 5 commandments on how to time travel properly.

ABIGATRA:

Like Thou Shall Not Teleport To the Beginning of Time.

ELIQUIS:

(*with emphasis*). Thou Shall Not Use This Machine To Switch Genders

ABIGATRA:

A time traveling machine can do that?

ELIQUIS:

Anything is possible

ABIGATRA:

These breasts are not real.

ELIQUIS:

I don't see any breasts. That machine is pretty flat-chested. And, a non-hairy one to boot!

ABIGATRA:

Moron, I meant I used to be a man.

ELIQUIS:

How long ago was that?

ABIGATRA:

Seven years ago.

ELIQUIS:

You have only been a woman for seven years?

ABIGATRA:

It's not like I can stretch it any longer.

ELIQUIS:

So? What can we do?

ABIGATRA:

Nothing now.

ELIQUIS:

I don't want to say—

ABIGATRA:

But yes, I have regrets.

ELIQUIS:

Once you have been operated on—

ABIGATRA:

It's hard to reverse engineer.

ELIQUIS:

Do you think it is harder for the time machine to revert back to an x-ray machine? Or vice versa? Once it makes the full transformation?

ABIGATRA:

My penis was hacked off. So, I think that can't be undone.

ELIQUIS:
> Why must one match the inside with the outside?

ABIGATRA:
> We are not meant to be born color-coded and color-coordinated.

ELIQUIS:
> Or are we?

ABIGATRA:
> Well, it was so clear to me what had to be done then.

ELIQUIS:
> To your body?

ABIGATRA:
> Exactly.

ELIQUIS:
> A flawless request.

ABIGATRA:
> Unerroneously.

ELIQUIS:
> Then what happened?

ABIGATRA:
> I have the urge to return to the past.

ELIQUIS:
> You miss your masculinity.

ABIGATRA:
> And, this new yearning can't be compromised.

ELIQUIS:
> So there is a time machine in you, your body, that wants to time-travel back to the epoch of its origin?

ABIGATRA:
> Well, the truth is….

ELIQUIS:
> You've been fighting so hard to become—

ABIGATRA:
> Who I did not want to be.

ELIQUIS:
> That's alarming.

ABIGATRA:
> Is it pride? Or blunder that's keeping me here.

ELIQUIS:
> With the x-ray machine?

ABIGATRA:
> With my unwanted self.

ELIQUIS:
> Maybe you should wait.

ABIGATRA:
> For God.

ELIQUIS:
> God. No. Wait before you change your mind. Again.

ABIGATRA:
> But I didn't change my mind.

ELIQUIS:
> But you said 'blunder' and 'unwanted self.'

ABIGATRA:
> Once there was this x-ray machine in me.

ELIQUIS:
> Before it became a time machine.

ABIGATRA:
> Yes.

ELIQUIS:
> That was always taking electromagnetic photographs.

ABIGATRA:
> Of my psychoanalytical body.

ELIQUIS:
> Basically, your sofa.

ABIGATRA:
> (*relieved*). No. My depression.

ELIQUIS:
> Pardon me?

ABIGATRA:
> I was troubled. Suicidal. In pain.

ELIQUIS:
> What do you mean?

ABIGATRA:
> There was a chemical imbalance in me.

ELIQUIS:
> Your binary voices fighting each other to maintain one voice.

ABIGATRA:
> Yes. And, that final voice manifested as gender.

ELIQUIS:
> It made you feel and be entirely female.

ABIGATRA:
> More truthfully, the x-ray machine in me was taking photographs of my depression so fast that I ended up time traveling.

ELIQUIS:
> (*laughing*). The cinema of your unhappiness warped time and space.

ABIGATRA:
> Rather, its velocity.

WAITING FOR GOD

ELIQUIS:

So you did not alter your mind.

ABIGATRA:

(*particularly*). Is my body my mind?

Silence. They appear static, heads influential, eyes dashed, baggy at the elbows.

ELIQUIS:

(*weakly*). Is your mind your body? (*Silence.*) Listen, where is the arrow of time in this—

ABIGATRA:

Let's pay full attention!

They eavesdrop by pressing their ears against the machine, incongruously inelastic in their postures.

ELIQUIS:

Where is your maleness now?

ABIGATRA:

Not sure. (*They eavesdrop.* ELIQUIS's *face grows hot from the machine. She gazes at* ABIGATRA, *who has her eyes closed so she can listen better.*) But I miss pissing standing up.

ELIQUIS:

What about shaving your face?

ABIGATRA:

That too.

ELIQUIS:

What else?

ABIGATRA:

Scratching my back.

ELIQUIS:

But that's gender-neutral.

ABIGATRA:
> No. Gender encompassing!

ELIQUIS:
> Taking a shower.

ABIGATRA:
> Anyone could do that!
>
> *Silence.*

ELIQUIS:
> (*fiercely*). Are you sure? You need a bath.

ABIGATRA:
> I need a showerhead pressed against my body.

ELIQUIS:
> Tell me no more!

ABIGATRA:
> It's not that sexual and I miss it regardless of what sex I choose to be.

ELIQUIS:
> It's time to put my shirt back on. (ABIGATRA *walks around a bit to find her shirt and when she sees it, she picks it up.* ELIQUIS *grabs it from her. Nippily*). Now that I am no longer gender-neutral in my head.

ABIGATRA:
> (*in disbelief*). But you already have a shirt on.

ELIQUIS:
> How should you know? You are not me. (*She digs again in her pouches, withdraws something from it. That something is nothing.*)

ABIGATRA:
> You won't find your shirt in those! Too small and it's

already on you. (*She continues to grope its interiority.*) At any rate, do you have my shirt? (*She digs deeper.*) Wait, I have it. Am I a magician of memory or am I not?

ELIQUIS:

You are a moron! And godless.

ABIGATRA:

(*surprised*). God. Yes! How is God, by the way?

ELIQUIS:

The question is, where is God?

ABIGATRA:

No. No. A better question…(*Silence.*) Why are we waiting for God?

ELIQUIS:

There was a reason why we're waiting for him. (*Silence.*) So scandalous (*She studies the nonexistent shirt admiringly, suspends it in the air with thumb and pinky.*) Right, right. (*She lifts and places the nonexistent shirt into her mouth wistfully.*) Hmmmmm…

ABIGATRA:

We're waiting because God commanded us to.

ELIQUIS:

(*her mouth stuffed with pretentious nothing, stupidly*). Hmmmm…

ABIGATRA:

Remove that stupid shirt from your mouth so I can hear you.

ELIQUIS:

(*masticates the shirtless air, gulps*). Isn't God omnipresent?

ABIGATRA:

Why did you swallow my shirt?

ELIQUIS:

When did it become yours?

ABIGATRA:

If God is everywhere, why are we asked to wait for him?

ELIQUIS:

Maybe he's busy?

ABIGATRA:

With what?

ELIQUIS:

Seducing women.

ABIGATRA:

That's an unfortunate vice to have (*Silence.*) For the moment.

ELIQUIS:

For us.

ABIGATRA:

Who could he be seducing?

ELIQUIS:

Princess Semele. (*She holds an invisible button in the light, up high, then tosses it in the air.*) Apparently, I didn't eat everything.

ABIGATRA:

Who is she?

ELIQUIS:

One of Zeus's mistresses.

ABIGATRA:

I thought we're waiting for a Christian god, you know, the one from one of the Abrahamic faiths?

ELIQUIS:

(*after sustained contemplation*). Do you want to stop waiting?

WAITING FOR GOD

Now that we might be waiting for a different God.

ABIGATRA:

Well, the message didn't really sectorize which God right?

ELIQUIS:

It could be Allah.

ABIGATRA:

It could. But if Allah programmed the message, he wouldn't? Would he?

ELIQUIS:

Wouldn't what?

ABIGATRA:

Use someone else's name instead of his own name.

ELIQUIS:

But it is essentially the same name.

ABIGATRA:

Right. Right.

ELIQUIS:

Maybe he programmed so it was limited to just 10 letters. No more. Allah would make it twelve.

ABIGATRA:

Look at how smart you are!

ELIQUIS:

No. No. How anti-Islamic of God. But, most importantly, why is he not here?

ABIGATRA:

(*nonchalantly*). Too busy seducing.

ELIQUIS:

Princess Semele.

ABIGATRA:
> Was she young and pretty?

ELIQUIS:
> Don't know.

ABIGATRA:
> She has to be.

ELIQUIS:
> Well. God—

ABIGATRA:
> Zeus!

ELIQUIS:
> Right. Right. Zeus had a hard time keeping his hands to himself. Hera was attractive, and being the immortal that she is, she didn't even age, but Zeus (*eyebrows lifting*)—

ABIGATRA:
> Like Matt Lauer, was ambitious down there.

ELIQUIS:
> Maybe too ambitious? At any rate, Hera got jealous and, spoiler, Semele, the mortal, got pregnant.

ABIGATRA:
> And Hera hired the enigmatic Jessica Jones to investigate?

ELIQUIS:
> Well, no. She read too many versions of *Beauty and the Beast* and it inspired her to befriend Semele by cloaking herself as an old, destitute woman, carrying a red perennial rose.

ABIGATRA:
> She wasn't carrying any rose. Let alone perennial!

ELIQUIS:
>(*exasperated*). Okay. Okay. Fine. No rose.

ABIGATRA:
>So…. to enact her revenge…

ELIQUIS:
>Semele spilled her guts to her new friend, telling Hera what an amazing lover Zeus was, how they were documenting their lovemaking sessions using Snapchat and Walala. One day, at a vegan pizza party, and at the height of her covetous intolerability, Hera convinced gullible Semele to take their fucking to a new height.

ABIGATRA:
>Oh, Hera is so devious.

ELIQUIS:
>(*excitedly*). The patience that woman has! She rallied Semele. 'Semele! I think your lover is holding back. He could give you so so much more. Do you want to fuck The Hulk or Bruce Banner? Do you want superhero sex or do you want normal, homo sapien sex?'

ABIGATRA:
>That must have been a difficult choice.

ELIQUIS:
>Well, naturally, superhero big is better, right?

ABIGATRA:
>(*clarifying*). From the standpoint of sex.

ELIQUIS:
>(*agitated*). What other standpoint is there? So to convince Zeus to fuck her in his unmasked form, Semele whispered lustfully to Zeus, 'I find it so sexy when a

man is completely naked with me. Won't you fuck my brains out in your raw, unhindered masculine form? Please. Please?'

ABIGATRA:

Well. Did it work?

ELIQUIS:

Maybe too well. After the third please, Zeus grew weak, but being the mortal that she was, her lack of experience with supernatural force in bed was telling. Semele couldn't handle its prodigious intensity—

ABIGATRA:

She figuratively exploded?

ELIQUIS:

She literally blew up!

ABIGATRA:

From sex.

ELIQUIS:

From trepidation, and she was scattered about in fragments, strands of her hair here, her eyeball there, her left torso down there, legs and arms tossed—

ABIGATRA:

Having sex with Zeus was like stepping on a landmine.

ELIQUIS:

For her. As his lover was dismantled in fleshly pieces, irreparable damage even for a God, Zeus realized he could still save the child. He yanked and transplanted their unborn six-month fetus from her womb and superglued the pre-natal embryonic lump onto his thigh to keep the fetus alive.

ABIGATRA:
And, not his back or belly?

ELIQUIS:
Thigh is a euphemism for his cock.

ABIGATRA:
(*flabbergasted*). God. Is his member muscular enough to hold the weight of a nine or so pound child?

ELIQUIS:
Well, he is God after all.

ABIGATRA:
Still, it is mightily unpleasant walking around with a human dumbbell attached to the most sensitive organ in the body.

ELIQUIS:
Nonetheless, it was worth it. That child turned out to be Dionysus.

ABIGATRA:
Poor Dionysus. Having to grow up in that way.

ELIQUIS:
Oh, don't pity him. He is Lord of Absinthe and Ecstasy. He is living *the* life.

ABIGATRA:
The most opulent kind then.

ELIQUIS:
Obviously.

ABIGATRA:
The fundamental hasn't altered.

ELIQUIS:
Our hands are tied, not quick enough. (*She pulls the*

nonexistent sleeve of a shirt to ABIGATRA.) Would you like to eat the rest of my shirt?

A horrendous yelp near them forces ELIQUIS *to lose her grip on the invisible shirt. They persist to linger without moving, then they each bolt in separate directions.* ELIQUIS *halts midway, walks very very slowly towards the center of the page, collects the undetectable shirt, crumples it into a ball and inserts it into her pants, walks back very slowly to greet* ABIGATRA *who is expecting her to stay still. Nestled as one cluster of silhouette, knees trembling, recoiling from the unknown threat, they stare.*

Enter KOHLRABI *and* NGỦ. KOHLRABI *commands* NGỦ *by zapping his collar with a small contraption in his hand.* NGỦ *arrives first because he is an animal (a slave and a goat), shadowed by* KOHLRABI. NGỦ *is lugging a large tool kit strapped on his back, a laptop, and one blue suitcase,* KOHLRABI *a doorbell.*

KOHLRABI:

Go! (*Fissure of electricity.* KOHLRABI *emerges. They walk across the page.* NGỦ *stands in front of* ABIGATRA *and* ELIQUIS. KOHLRABI *notices* ABIGATRA *and* ELIQUIS. *The noise of the electricity current fizzles out.* KOHLRABI *grips the contraption tightly.*) Stop!

The strap snaps and the contents collapse around NGỦ. ABIGATRA *and* ELIQUIS *rush towards him, indecisive about what to do.* ABIGATRA *makes the first move towards*

NGỦ, *who has already fallen asleep.* ELIQUIS *pushes* ABIGATRA *forward so that she launches and nearly falls.*

ABIGATRA:

Why did you push me?

ELIQUIS:

To give you a good head start.

KOHLRABI:

Tread lightly! Don't go too near. (ABIGATRA *and* ELIQUIS *face* KOHLRABI.) He's judgmental.

ELIQUIS:

(*sotto voce*). Is that who I think it is?

ABIGATRA:

Monotheistic conception.

ELIQUIS:

(*having a moment of amnesia, confused*). What . . .?

ABIGATRA:

God.

ELIQUIS:

No.

KOHLRABI:

Kohlrabi here.

ABIGATRA:

(*to* ELIQUIS). I don't think so.

ELIQUIS:

I was referring to the goat.

ABIGATRA:

(*incredulously*). You really think that goat is God?

ELIQUIS:

(*unobtrusively, to* KOHLRABI). Mr. German Turnip,

(*points to the goat*). Who is he?

KOHLRABI:

(*petrifying non-Germanic accent*). I am KOHLRABI! (*Silence.*) Kohlrabi! (*Silence.*) Kohlrabi. (*Silence.*) How edible am I? (*Silence.*) Have you eaten me before?

ABIGATRA and ELIQUIS *stare at their surroundings inquisitively.*

ELIQUIS:

(*feigning confusion*). Cabbage . . . Kale . . .Cauliflower....

ABIGATRA:

Kohlrabi . . . kohlrabi . . .

KOHLRABI:

NGỦ!

ELIQUIS:

I see! Kohlrabi . . . broccoli . . . kohlrabi . . .

ABIGATRA:

Which is it: kohlrabi or broccoli?

ELIQUIS:

Kohlrabi . . . possibly . . . not sure...I mean....should I know?

KOHLRABI *approaches them inauspiciously.*

ABIGATRA:

(*placating*). Kohlrabi is an imperative influence of the Kashmiri gastronomy...

ELIQUIS:

(*impulsively*). We don't know how you were born or why you have arrived to us, Mr. German Turnip.

KOHLRABI:

(*firmly*). Atheists you are, eh? (*He whips out his monocle.*)

I could smell your anti-God odor from afar. (*He places the monocle over his eye.*) Let me inspect you. (*He giggles quietly to himself.*) An identical product as this fancy cabbage! Born from the ground up.

ABIGATRA:

Er…not quite—

KOHLRABI:

(*dogmatically*). What do you want?

ELIQUIS:

God.

KOHLRABI:

You are supposed to be atheists.

ABIGATRA:

Well….we're getting there.

KOHLRABI:

But not yet?

ABIGATRA:

We are…. waiting…. you know… to find out… potentially… if God really wants us to be atheists. (*making things up because she is nervous*).

ELIQUIS:

It's a weird thing we do…

ABIGATRA:

I wouldn't recommend it … it's not profitable.….

ELIQUIS:

Why are you here?

KOHLRABI:

Someone sent me here.

ABIGATRA:

Who?

KOHLRABI:

Find my laptop and I will show it to you!

ABIGATRA *and* ELIQUIS *stare at each other in confusion.*

ELIQUIS & ABIGATRA:

(*in unison*). What is a laptop?

KOHLRABI:

It's a portable computer. Were you born yesterday?

ABIGATRA:

Absolutely not.

ELIQUIS:

Maybe the day before yesterday.

KOHLRABI:

When were you both born?

ABIGATRA:

We came from the 6th dimension.

ELIQUIS:

And, we are still in the 6th dimension.

KOHLRABI:

That's a place, not when.

ELIQUIS:

It's both, where time and space is one.

ABIGATRA:

That's how we see things nowadays.

ELIQUIS:

Where time is space. Space is time.

KOHLRABI:

That's a scandal!

ELIQUIS:

(*flinching before* KOHLRABI). You were saying . . . about . . . who delivered you. . . .

KOHLRABI:
> Yes, yes.

ELIQUIS:
> And....

KOHLRABI:
> Find my laptop!

ELIQUIS:
> What does it look like?

KOHLRABI:
> Flat and black and rectangular.

ABIGATRA:
> Like a flat piece of paper?

KOHLRABI:
> But fatter and thicker and sleeker.
>
> *Both* ELIQUIS *and* ABIGATRA *rummage about the fallen objects surrounding* NGŮ. ELIQUIS *lifts up a heavy bag.*

ELIQUIS:
> (*out of breath*). I think I found it!

ABIGATRA:
> (*with a black object in hand*). I got it!

KOHLRABI:
> (*pointing at them*). YOU! Bring it to me.
>
> *They both stare at each other.*

ELIQUIS:
> Her or me?

KOHLRABI:
> (*to* ELIQUIS). not you, her!

ELIQUIS:
> That is Abigatra. I call her Gatra.

KOHLRABI:
>And, you?

ELIQUIS:
>I am Eliquis.

KOHLRABI:
>Eliquis. Eliquis… hmmm…

ELIQUIS:
>I am a type of blood thinner.

KOHLRABI:
>(*bored*). Er….

ELIQUIS:
>I stop blood from clotting. And, sometimes pulmonary embolism.

KOHLRABI:
>Your parents have a strange sense of humor.

ELIQUIS:
>Actually, Prophetess Isaiah named me.

KOHLRABI:
>You mean Jewish Prophet Isaiah.

ELIQUIS:
>No no. Prophetess Isaiah.

KOHLRABI:
>(*elated with certainty*). Who is she if not 8th-century BC and vegetarian?

ELIQUIS:
>She is the leader of the 6th dimension and not vegetarian!

ABIGATRA:
>She's really wise, really loves goat meat, and can

prognosticate the future.

KOHLRABI:

Because she foresaw your future so she named you?

ELIQUIS:

No, no. She names all children born from RW.

ABIGATRA:

It's a Robot Womb, Mr. German Turnip.

KOHLRABI:

No wonder you don't know what a laptop is. May I have it, Gatra?

(ABIGATRA *hands the laptop over to him*. KOHLRABI *squats on the floor to open it. Then he places the doorbell next to the DELETE key*).

ABIGATRA:

Why does your laptop need a doorbell?

KOHLRABI:

Well, that's how I can access the computer.

ABIGATRA:

Will a person come to your door to open it?

(ELIQUIS *and* ABIGATRA *squat next to* KOHLRABI.)

KOHLRABI:

No, its memory will appear.

ELIQUIS:

Passwords are ancient for us too.

KOHLRABI:

How do you access things then?

ABIGATRA:

Our entire body is a password. We can't ever be replicated, even when thieves and murderers clone us.

KOHLRABI:

What if you lose your leg, you won't be able to access anything?

ABIGATRA:

That's a great question. I've never lost a body part before.

(*A video of a burning bush appears on the laptop screen.*)

ELIQUIS:

It's a burning bush!

ABIGATRA:

A digital thornbush.

ELIQUIS:

(*speechless*). An ignited bush sent you here?

ABIGATRA:

Why does this feel so biblical?

ELIQUIS:

(*staring at* KOHLRABI *in amazement*). You are not Moses, are you?

KOHLRABI:

No! Of course not. I am Kohlrabi.

ABIGATRA:

(*pointing to* NGỦ, *the goat, still asleep*). That thing.

KOHLRABI:

Yes…

ABIGATRA:

Isn't God, right?

KOHLRABI:

No no. Why would you think that? That is NGỦ. It means sleep in Vietnamese.

WAITING FOR GOD

ELIQUIS:

Maybe you should have named him Thức.

ABIGATRA:

But that hasn't explained why you have arrived here, Mr. German Turnip.

KOHLRABI:

Before coming here, I had a vision.

ELIQUIS:

(*appalled*). You hallucinated your way towards us?

KOHLRABI:

(*with a philanthropic wave*). Not important. (*He holds tight to the contraption.*) Wake up sheep! (*Silence.*) He spends his entire existence lethargic. (*Zaps the collar*). Shake it up lamb! (NGỦ *gabbles with the sleek ground.* KOHLRABI *zaps the collar.*) Up! (NGỦ *slumps.*) Get up! (NGỦ *immobile*). Now! (NGỦ *pushes his entire weight vertically. To* ABIGATRA *and* ELIQUIS, *cordially*). Mademoiselles, my pointless life is ardently ignited by your presence. (*They respond with skeptical facial expressions.*) Of course, genuinely exultant. (*He zaps the collar.*) Upright! (NGỦ *trots two steps backward.*) Forward! (NGỦ *takes two more steps backward.*) Life is a series of empty, vacant cards. A deckful of hearts and diamonds . . . (*he looks at his timeless wrist*) . . . hmmm . . . (*he analyzes*) . . . and yet, I still have a few tricks up my sleeves (*To* NGỦ). Release! (NGỦ *expels several dark pancake-size dungs from his goat's ass.*) No more! (KOHLRABI *zaps the collar.* NGỦ *expels several more dark defecated pancakes while* KOHLRABI *zaps him.* KOHLRABI *walks towards his tool kit.*) What did I tell you? No more! (NGỦ *collapses on the ground and falls asleep while* KOHLRABI *zaps him into wakefulness, but as his name indicates faithfully, sleeping is his ontological composition.*) It seems like winter might be coming (KOHLRABI *looks up and down, then sideways, then he begins to cry.*) All he does is sleep and shit. (NGỦ *wakes up, and with all of his effort, lifts his entire goatly body up while* KOHLRABI *wipes tears from his eyes.* NGỦ *lets out an animal cough before falling back asleep.*) Yes, Mademoiselles, I am a stone that learns how to weep for the first time, (*he places the monocle on the ledge of his upper cheek and scrutinizes the ladies*) especially when other more lachrymose stones won't weep with me. (*He removes his monocle.*) Hallelujah! (NGỦ *startles awake and bolts up into a standing position, all four hooves on the ground before trotting up and down the page*) Imbecile! (NGỦ *stops trotting and comes to a complete standstill, sneezes, and then collapses from exhaustion.* KOHLRABI *walks over to his suitcase, unzips it, and pulls out a kohlrabi, two dried whole whitefish, a handkerchief, one loaf of bread, a bottle of rum, three paper cups, and throws some sundried grasshoppers over to* NGỦ *where it lands on his head with a thump.*) Eat! (NGỦ, *undisturbed.*) Don't be a poor guest. (NGỦ *yawns with his goat mouth wide open.*) Don't! It's contagious. (NGỦ *closes his mouth. To* ABIGATRA *and* ELIQUIS.) Since you won't cry with me, Mademoiselles, won't you feast with me before I fulfill your darkest fantasies with my portable computer? EAT! (NGỦ, *deeply asleep, immobile.*) Have some, ladies, this biblical dish that God so generously offers us. (*He extends the whitefish to* ELIQUIS,

WAITING FOR GOD

offers the loaf of bread to ABIGATRA, *and lastly, he uncorks the bottle of rum.*) Please! (NGŮ *finally snores.* ELIQUIS *tears a piece of whitefish and* ABIGATRA *breaks the bread open while* KOHLRABI *pours them each some rum.*) Don't be shy! (KOHLRABI *unfolds the handkerchief and places it over the pile of dungs.*) The smell of the air is so wonderful, ain't it? *They all eat in silence.*

ABIGATRA *and* ELIQUIS *vigilantly study* NGŮ *before approaching him, examining him horizontally and vertically until there are no more shades of his existence left unturned.* KOHLRABI *masticates a* kohlrabi *ravenously while discarding hard bits that couldn't be chewed from its inedible, unlikeable exterior.* NGŮ *attempts standing up, but finds no purpose and soon falls fast asleep. Once in a while,* KOHLRABI *takes a break from his chewing and zaps him. Despite the zapping,* NGŮ *remains motionless.*

ELIQUIS:
> (*chewing*). For everyone's sake, I hope that goat isn't God.

ABIGATRA:
> It isn't a good way to treat anyone, let alone a supreme being.

ELIQUIS:
> (*quietly*). I mean I hope this isn't his way of answering our prayers.

ABIGATRA:
> If he is God in disguise, he could hear you no matter how softly you speak.

ELIQUIS:

(*tossing the fish bone into the air*). Do you think each zap is a prayer from a human?

ABIGATRA:

(*chewing*). Maybe he doesn't know what to do with our prayers, so he shits and then sleeps.

ELIQUIS:

(*putting another fish piece into her mouth*). He can't be God. He just can't.

ABIGATRA:

In the master and slave counternarrative, the slaves are the authoritative figures. The masters display obedience and are the true servants of society.

ELIQUIS:

Look at Jesus, Lord and Messiah of man, washing the dirty feet of his disciples. Those who are kings or who lead *serve* those who are not.

ABIGATRA:

Based on this theory, the goat has to be God. Kohlrabi who zaps him all the time is Moses.

ABIGATRA:

(*pointing*). No. That's stupid. God has to be in that laptop, behind that digital burning thornbush.

ELIQUIS:

Kohlrabi can't be Moses. Just look at the way he eats.

ABIGATRA:

(*Pulling a piece of fish stuck in between her teeth*). How does he eat?

ELIQUIS:

(*exasperated*). Can't you see? Like a starving child.

ABIGATRA:

Moses doesn't?

ELIQUIS:

Despite being born as an enslaved Israeli, Moses was adopted by the Princess of Egypt and raised in a Kardashian-like household, so of course, he doesn't eat like that.

ABIGATRA:

In the original biblical text, God talks to Moses on Mount Horeb by being the burning bush, right?

ELIQUIS *comes closer to* ABIGATRA.

ELIQUIS:

(*near shouting into her ear*). He *is* the burning bush!

ABIGATRA:

I guess if you have something important to say—

ELIQUIS:

You get burnt up and hide in a bush to say it.

ABIGATRA:

I mean, where else would you hide yourself in the desert?

ELIQUIS:

At any rate, where is he? Hiding from us?

ABIGATRA:

(*tearing the fish apart with her fingers*). Taking preemptive measures.

ELIQUIS:

The kingdom expects this foresight.

ABIGATRA:

He's too busy schooling his son on how to foil Satan from gaslighting him.

ELIQUIS:
>He could still teach Jesus that and show up here for us.

ABIGATRA:
>(*rancorously*). Maybe he's already multi-tasking. Coaching his son in anti-Satanic combat moves AND trying to talk him out of flying too high. With feathers made out of wax, his wings would melt.

ELIQUIS:
>(*shaking her head, impish expression*). Poor Icarus. This is why I'm not going to have any sons!

ABIGATRA:
>But if I had to choose a father to learn from…

ELIQUIS:
>I'd choose God over Zeus.

ABIGATRA:
>I wouldn't choose either. Both of their sons died!

ELIQUIS:
>That's very telling of the fathers.

ABIGATRA:
>Icarus from drowning and the Messiah from impalement.

ELIQUIS:
>Exactly.

ABIGATRA:
>But is it the fathers's fault?

ELIQUIS:
>Does it matter?

ABIGATRA:
>One son heeded his father's advice.

ELIQUIS:
>And, the other didn't.

ABIGATRA:
>Yet, both dead. Very young.

ELIQUIS:
>We can't blame their demise purely because they're young.

ABIGATRA:
>I wasn't implying that they died because they were young.

ELIQUIS:
>I know. I know.

ABIGATRA:
>They died but they also happened to be young.

ELIQUIS:
>(*apologetically*). I mean....Icarus....

ABIGATRA:
>Just blurt it out!

ELIQUIS:
>(*overtly vocal*). Do you think Icarus had bipolar?

ELIQUIS:
>You think he didn't listen to his father because he had a brain disorder?

ABIGATRA:
>Yeah. Yeah. Maybe he flew too high because he was feeling high and manic.

ELIQUIS:
>Too gleeful in a bad way.

ABIGATRA:
>He could have flown low too, near the sea, which would macerate his feathers.

ELIQUIS:

In which case, just as treacherous, he died anyway by drowning.

ABIGATRA:

Either way, he was fucked.

ELIQUIS:

That's what bipolarity can do to ya.

ABIGATRA:

So do you blame him or the disease?

ELIQUIS:

(*supremely alarmed*). Oh. My. God.

ABIGATRA:

What is it?

ELIQUIS:

Fuck us.

ABIGATRA:

Spit it out!

ELIQUIS:

I don't think Zeus was Icarus's father.

ABIGATRA:

Who is then?

ELIQUIS:

(*searching mentally*). The Athenian inventor….er…Die….er…

ABIGATRA:

Daedra?

ELIQUIS:

(*triumphantly*). Daedalus!

ABIGATRA:

How could you confuse a mere mortal with mighty Zeus?

ELIQUIS:

Well, you are to blame too.

ABIGATRA:

I got carried away by the comparison.

ELIQUIS:

I was thinking actually of Phaeton when I thought of Icarus.

ABIGATRA:

But still, Zeus wasn't his father.

ELIQUIS:

Helios was. The God of the Sun.

ABIGATRA:

My point.

ELIQUIS:

At any rate, would you pour boiling water onto your enemy?

ABIGATRA:

It depends on who my enemy is.

ELIQUIS:

Someone who is greedy.

ABIGATRA:

No.

ELIQUIS:

Why not?

ABIGATRA:

Not egregious enough of a crime.

ELIQUIS:

Well.

ABIGATRA:

Well.

ELIQUIS:

Daedalus slayed Minos by pouring scorching water fresh from the kettle onto him.

ABIGATRA:

Was he clothed?

ELIQUIS:

Butt naked, in the middle of taking a bath.

ABIGATRA:

Would you want a father who used hot water that way?

KOHLRABI:

Don't intrude on his life! (*They rotate their bodies, facing KOHLRABI who has taken a large gulp from the bottle of rum*) I'm sure he has his reasons for torturing, slaughtering him. (*He takes another gigantic gulp from his rum bottle. ELIQUIS observes the pile of food waste and mess surrounding him. NGŮ remains soporific. KOHLRABI clangs the bottle against the ground and zaps his collar. NGŮ shakes his legs and hooves in the air, but eyes remain closed. ELIQUIS is fixated by the commotion. KOHLRABI lifts the bottle in the air and takes another defiant gulp.*) He wanted to vent—

ELIQUIS:

(*faint-heartedly*). What?

KOHLRABI:

His son died in a terrible way and he probably didn't know how to cope with it.

ELIQUIS:

Are you making excuses for him?

ABIGATRA:

(*magnified*). He's saving the last drop of rum for us.

KOHLRABI:

I am somebody's brother.

ELIQUIS:

Who?

KOHLRABI:

Not Cain's brother, Abel.

ABIGATRA:

Are you bitter?

KOHLRABI:

Never. I am Kohlrabi. I am so sweet. (ELIQUIS *moves closer to him*). The world loves me, it does, including God. When I returned from the Afghan war, my daughter did not greet me at the doorstep, nor collapse in my arms and perish like Jephthah's daughter… (ELIQUIS *retreats where she is closer to* ABIGATRA) . . . instead I found my brother in bed with my wife.

ELIQUIS *and* ABIGATRA *hug each other.*

ELIQUIS:

Are you sure the world loves you?

ABIGATRA:

(*pinching* ELIQUIS). Your definition of love is very progressive, Mr. German Turnip!

KOHLRABI:

Aye. Aye. (*To* ELIQUIS). I stir easily like a stone.

ELIQUIS:

Are you no longer on speaking terms with your brother? (NGÙ *gazes up from his slumber.*)

KOHLRABI:

Why wouldn't we be? (*To* NGÙ). Go back to where you belong.

ABIGATRA:
(*shocked*). You forgave her?
KOHLRABI:
What crime did she commit? Is missing me a crime?
ELIQUIS:
(*eyes bulging*). She slept with your brother.
KOHLRABI:
She said she missed me so much when I was at war and sleeping with my brother could only alleviate her pain. By the way, my brother, though we're not twins, looks exactly like me.
ABIGATRA:
How sacrificing of your brother.
ELIQUIS:
(*tapping her head*). The war didn't knock a few loose screws in there?
ABIGATRA:
Where were you when Cain and Abel were born?
KOHLRABI:
(*confused*). Help me understand.
ABIGATRA:
Both Cain and Abel, after months of arduous harvest and shepherding, offer their oblations to God.
ELIQUIS:
God gave Cain a cold shoulder and emotionally hugged Abel.
ABIGATRA:
Cain felt the pain of God's favoritism, and soon after, found Abel and slaughtered him.

KOHLRABI:
So soon?
ELIQUIS:
I would have waited.
ABIGATRA:
For what?
ELIQUIS:
(*exasperated*). For a time to interrogate God! Why else?
KOHLRABI:
Like what you are doing here?
ABIGATRA:
(*being reasonable*). Well. God didn't actually reject our sacrifice.
KOHLRABI:
Well, not showing up is like giving a cold shoulder.
ABIGATRA:
We assume.
ELIQUIS:
But we don't really know if God made this appointment with us.
KOHLRABI:
And, if he actually shows up, what would you ask him?
ABIGATRA:
Why did you rebuff Cain's loving sacrifice?
ELIQUIS:
(*rolling eyes*). Why would you ask him something we could deduce logically?
ABIGATRA:
But we don't really know the answer.

KOHLRABI:
> (*siding with* ELIQUIS). She has a point, why would a reasonable God take sides unless it has arrived from a place of prudence?

ELIQUIS:
> But was God shrewd and sensible when he embarrassed him in front of his brother?

ABIGATRA:
> It made Cain feel less loved.

KOHLRABI:
> I see, resulting in Cain's murderous response.

ELIQUIS:
> Quite literally!

ABIGATRA:
> But God could have pre-de-escalated the situation.

KOHLRABI:
> By what?

ELIQUIS:
> Taking Cain aside, near a bush, away from Abel.

ABIGATRA:
> And asking him, 'Hey, son, why did you not offer your best akebia quinate to me? Why did you offer your overripe strawberries and spoiled mandarins? Why would you offer me less than what I deserve?'

KOHLRABI:
> (*appalled*). He gave God rotten gifts?

ELIQUIS:
> That penny pincher!

ABIGATRA:
> Well, he reasoned since God technically doesn't eat.

WAITING FOR GOD

ELIQUIS:

So it doesn't make any sense to offer him the best.

ABIGATRA:

When it could go to waste.

KOHLRABI:

For thinking more eco-friendly and being economically prudent, God shunned him?

ELIQUIS:

Well.

ABIGATRA:

Since you put it that way…

KOHLRABI:

God being God—

ELIQUIS:

(*inspired*). He would have given the gifts back to them.

ABIGATRA:

Knowing that they needed them for survival.

KOHLRABI:

So the oblation was purely symbolic?

ELIQUIS:

Not quite. One must be iconic in one's futility!

ABIGATRA:

He was trying to teach them both that when they offered the best of the best of their labor…

ELIQUIS:

To him, that they are giving themselves the best too! As karma dictates it, the gifts would have come right back to them.

ABIGATRA:

Abel got the lesson.

KOHLRABI:

Cain was slow.

ELIQUIS:

But what I don't get is, yes, Cain wasn't God's best student, but why punish him so cruelly?

KOHLRABI:

He killed one of the earliest citizens of Earth. God's favorite too.

ABIGATRA:

He was marked in a way that no one could even end his misery by snuffing him out too soon nor too prematurely.

KOHLRABI:

(*sympathetic*). The punishment more than exceeded the crime.

ELIQUIS:

As if God was out to get him.

ABIGATRA:

(*curious*). What was his torture?

KOHLRABI:

Ask her!

ELIQUIS:

Perpetual fugitive.

ABIGATRA:

Poor Cain.

KOHLRABI:

(*echoing each other*). I love him. I really do.

ABIGATRA:

(*echoing each other*). I love his dehumanization.

KOHLRABI:
(*echoing each other*). I love how defective he is.

ELIQUIS:
And rotten fruits tend to be more organic without synthetic fertilizers, don't you think?

ABIGATRA:
(*echoing each other*). I love how he lied to God about killing his brother.

KOHLRABI:
(*echoing each other*). I love how he is a farmer and has to till the land.

ABIGATRA:
(*echoing each other*). I love how he had to wander from year to year, with nothing to hope for.

ELIQUIS:
Oh, shut up you two! Stop romanticizing your love for him.

ABIGATRA:
This isn't romanticism.

ELIQUIS:
What is it then?

KOHLRABI:
We are just trying to imagine what it is like to love someone God wouldn't love.

ABIGATRA:
Someone has to do it.

ELIQUIS:
God did not not love Cain! Cain sinned against "God" by bringing an inaccurate sacrifice.

ABIGATRA:

What was he supposed to bring that was "accurate?"

ELIQUIS:

Something not rotten, to start?

ABIGATRA:

(*All three rotate their human figures towards* NGỦ). Where is God in all of this?

ELIQUIS:

Why won't he wake up instead of turning his ass towards us?

ABIGATRA:

(*quietly*). We can't assume that is him.

KOHLRABI:

Regardless of what God thinks, I love that Cain didn't know any better.

ABIGATRA:

(*echoing each other*). I love how he lied to God about killing his brother.

KOHLRABI:

(*echoing each other*). I love how, by killing his brother, his fucking options multiplied two fold! The only two women in the world. His sisters. Oh, his sisters!

ABIGATRA:

(*echoing each other*). No. No. No. The only other woman, his mother—

KOHLRABI:

(*echoing each other*). No. No. No. The only other woman, his mother—

ABIGATRA:

(*echoing each other*). Is ineligible.

KOHLRABI:

(*echoing each other*). Is ineligible.

ABIGATRA:

(*echoing each other*). Ineligible (*fading voice*).

KOHLRABI:

(*echoing each other*). Ineligible (*fading voice*).

ABIGATRA:

(*breaking that echo*). By the way, I love his female sin.

ELIQUIS:

What?

ABIGATRA:

You refute my love for his sin?

ELIQUIS:

You specified the sin.

ABIGATRA:

Someone has to do it.

ELIQUIS:

You said *female* sin.

ABIGATRA:

(*nonchalantly*). The sin is gendered. So?

ELIQUIS:

You want the word "sin" to twirl like a transsexual?

ABIGATRA:

Like me?

KOHLRABI:

I know in Hebrew the word for "sin" is feminine.

ELIQUIS:

Which I assume—

ABIGATRA:

(*being scandalous*). All male species are denied the privilege of committing sins.

KOHLRABI:

They cannot make a mistake ever! They are obviously saints.

ELIQUIS:

Obviously!

KOHLRABI:

You know (*silence*).... (*lowering his voice*). I just don't think Cain is capable of committing sin.

ELIQUIS:

(*whispering*). Because he is not female enough?

KOHLRABI:

Exactly.

ABIGATRA:

(*hearing it too clearly*). Will you two imbeciles just shut up? Everyone, male or female, beast or saint, is capable of committing sins.

ELIQUIS:

(*mercurial*). She's right you know. We're born to err!

ABIGATRA:

I don't know.

ELIQUIS:

(*philosophically*). Life is too short to err.

ABIGATRA:

I don't think Cain was thinking of brevity.

KOHLRABI:

What was he thinking then?

ABIGATRA:

Beauty.

KOHLRABI:

Beauty.

ELIQUIS:

Beauty.

ABIGATRA:

(*clarifying*). Cain was the oldest. And, because he was the oldest, he outranked Abel in spousal choice. Because God wasn't pleased with Cain's sacrifice, he demoted him.

KOHLRABI:

Cain and Abel both wanted the prettiest.

ELIQUIS:

Who doesn't?

ABIGATRA:

I don't. I like my men bald and hairy!

ELIQUIS:

Full of contradictions.

ABIGATRA:

How is it one? I like their skulls sleek like monks and their bodies, yee haw!, a forest fire of hair. That's my style.

KOHLRABI:

Just pile them. Just pile them up.

ELIQUIS:

I don't mean to diminish your sexual tastes, but of the two twin sisters, who was prettier!

KOHLRABI:

How should I know?

ELIQUIS:

Aclima or Awan?

ABIGATRA:

I don't know.

KOHLRABI:

Ask him (*eyes lifting, hinting towards* NGỦ).

They all approach NGỦ.

ABIGATRA:

(*bending over lightly*). Sir?

ELIQUIS:

(*bending*). God?

KOHLRABI:

(*shaking his body*). Ngủ. Wake up. Ngủ, wake up.

ELIQUIS:

How is he ever going to answer anyone's prayers if he's always that way?

ABIGATRA:

That's the only question that mysterious thing could answer.

KOHLRABI:

Wait a minute. I don't get it.

ABIGATRA:

What don't you get?

KOHLRABI:

If the sisters were twins, shouldn't their beauty be equally exact and similar? And symmetrical?

ELIQUIS:

They might not be identical.

ABIGATRA:

Regardless, why would the boys murderously bicker over a slight difference in beauty? It is in the same family of beauty.

KOHLRABI:

The only family.

ELIQUIS:
> It wasn't like they have other humans roaming about for comparison.

KOHLRABI:
> It's instinctual. It matters. It matters. Just answer me: who was prettier?

ELIQUIS:
> (*protective*). Don't answer that, Gatra!

KOHLRABI:
> It's harmless.

ELIQUIS:
> Lethal! The last time someone attempted to answer that superlative, it led to the catastrophic decade-long Trojan War.

ABIGATRA:
> I'm not even Paris.

ELIQUIS:
> You don't even need to be. You could be symbolically him.

KOHLRABI:
> Eh, a little over-cautious, young man?

ELIQUIS:
> Woman.

ABIGATRA:
> Just think about it. If God—

ELIQUIS:
> If Zeus had answered that quarrel in the first place instead of evading by re-assigning that task to a mere gorgeous-blind mortal like Paris, there wouldn't have been a war.

KOHLRABI:
A war was inevitable.
ABIGATRA:
A holy, godly war would have been the worst.
KOHLRABI:
Amongst the gods and goddesses, yes, indeed. All of mankind would perish from such a war.
ABIGATRA:
The second coming of Titanomachy.
ELIQUIS:
Titanomachy or not, personally, I think Athena is prettier.
KOHLRABI:
(*in raptures*). What about Aclima?
ELIQUIS:
What about her?
KOHLRABI:
(*in persuasion*). Ngủ! Ngủ (NGỦ *arcs his back.*) Who is more beautiful? (*Reticence of* NGỦ. *To* ELIQUIS). If he moves his front hooves first, it's Aclima. (ELIQUIS *blinks her eyes*). If he moves anything else, it has to be Awan.
ABIGATRA:
(*anxiously*). Sir! Is it Awan or Aclima? (*Long silence. No movement from* NGỦ. *Staggered*, KOHLRABI *stares back and forth between* ELIQUIS *and* ABIGATRA. ELIQUIS *ostensibly chill.* ABIGATRA *disconcerted*).
NGỦ:
HRRRRRRRRRRRR.
KOHLRABI:
(*To* NGỦ). What did you say?

WAITING FOR GOD

ABIGATRA:

(*quick to suggest*). Did he move?

ELIQUIS:

He said something, but he didn't even stir his tongue.

KOHLRABI:

If he moved his tongue, it would have been Awan!

ABIGATRA:

(*achingly*). Seeing him that way makes me feel so hopeless about Cain's future.

ELIQUIS:

Don't grieve, Gatra. Cain is already dead.

KOHLRABI:

In fact, God made sure his entire family line was completely obliterated from the consciousness of future time. (**KOHLRABI** *thumps the rum bottle against the ground. He gazes up at* NGŨ *to see if he stirs, but he is met with silence.*) How God thoroughly and devilishly punished Cain. And, he won't even wake up to defend his own cruelty to a child that knows no better. (*He contemplates.*) He even marked Cain's existence on earth in a way that he couldn't even end his own suffering via suicide. He could not even hire an assassin to slaughter him off the earth. (**ELIQUIS** *and* **ABIGATRA** *maintain their reticence.*) He wandered from one end of the earth in a constant state of homelessness. (*Stillness.*) How could one not have loved Cain? He's so easy to love. (*Groans.*) You know how life is. It's always dark. (*Stillness.*) And, when there's light. It doesn't last. Just a few seconds to let us know that we've been terrible fools (*Stillness.*)

Empty fools. They call it resilience for existing for so long, as long as I have. You know… I read *Jane Eyre* once not too long ago without knowing if day was night and—in what way shall I remark—without playing into the hopeless romantic trope… Sorry? (*Silence.*) Did somebody say something? (*Extended motionlessness.*) Even I, after so much tormented wandering, would have wanted someone, like Jane, drenched in macerated ash and soot, to come for me, emotionally blind, injured, and incomplete. Cain couldn't even have that. God made sure of it. (*His sadness morbidly infuses the air.*)

ELIQUIS:

Did God go too far?

KOHLRABI:

God was autistic when it comes to dispensing human pain.

ELIQUIS:

He just doesn't know when to stop.

ABIGATRA:

We can learn from this. If God doesn't wake up or come for us, we should just proceed without him.

ELIQUIS:

So soon?

KOHLRABI:

What is the urgency? (NGỦ *moves his hooves spectacularly quietly and the movement is cautiously not noticed by the three and soon enough, he is on his feet.*)

ABIGATRA:

(*fervidly*). Where will we go?

KOHLRABI:
> We have all the time in the world.

ABIGATRA:
> Not really.

KOHLRABI:
> I beg of you, what do you mean by that?

ELIQUIS:
> (*hopelessly*). It means it's time to give up on God.

KOHLRABI:
> (*taking the rum bottle*). Let me take a drink first . . . (*instead of pouring it into the drinking vessel, he holds the bottle in the air with confident wrist fitness and lets it drip down one fat ovoid drop at a time*) . . . before we ensue together. Life is a midget that we can't stretch to make her taller.

ELIQUIS:
> Who said you're joining us?

KOHLRABI:
> (*To* ABIGATRA.) You don't mind, do you? Sometimes I am human. Sometimes I am one of those machines that are missing a few parts. But I work all the same. Don't you want to touch me? (*To* ABIGATRA *and* ELIQUIS.) To see what I am made of before you gaze up at that other machine to measure and compare me? (*They turn to examine the x-ray machine.*) Excellent isn't it? (*They stare down at their feet.*) Let me talk to you about my brother. And, if you don't like what you hear about him, you can abandon me. (*He studies the rum bottles, inspects them.*) It's so unfortunate. Not one drop left. (*Clearing his throat.*) I'm the most important prophet in this Anthropocene.

I'm very peculiarly wise, but what do you know?

ELIQUIS:

Those who compliment the length and lusciousness of their tail are obnoxiously unwise.

KOHLRABI:

Only a cupcake would make such a spiteful remark.

ELIQUIS:

I'm no cupcake.

KOHLRABI:

You are fluffy and airy up there (*He taps the center of his head*) . . . and a round (*Tapping his own belly*) body filled with sugar, butter, and bad carbohydrates.

ELIQUIS:

Talk about someone with no substance.

KOHLRABI:

Stale cake.

ABIGATRA:

Stop it!

KOHLRABI:

(*charmed*). My great great great great great great grandfather...

ABIGATRA:

(*to* ELIQUIS). Listen.

ELIQUIS:

I am!

ABIGATRA:

(*to* KOHLRABI). You were saying about your father to the seventh power?

ELIQUIS:

He's not Nicolas Chuquet.

ABIGATRA:
> Let's pretend he is.

ELIQUIS:
> You're deserting me.

ABIGATRA:
> Completely out of line!

ELIQUIS:
> Our prophetess is superior.

ABIGATRA:
> Just listen. We're not comparing Trump with Marilyn vos Savant

KOHLRABI:
> Hello. I'm right here, you know. (KOHLRABI *has monitored this brief bantering with some detached engagement, knowing that knowledge can only be assuaged by mindless anecdotes*).

ABIGATRA:
> Indeed you are. Your father to the seventh power—

ELIQUIS:
> Is he important?

KOHLRABI:
> My super great grandfather is blind. And, his name is Tiresias.

ELIQUIS:
> Are you looking for him? Is this why you're mentioning him?

KOHLRABI:
> Well, it's hard to look for him.

ABIGATRA:
> Why is that?

ELIQUIS:

Did he murder someone? Is he in prison?

ABIGATRA:

Shush, Eliq! He's about to move his lips.

ELIQUIS *walks towards and stands next to* ABIGATRA. *Then, impatiently, they squat down and gaze up at* KOHLRABI.

KOHLRABI:

It never gets old, does it? (NGỬ *even strolls over, surprising the three.*) Even he's intrigued! (NGỬ *eyes him.*) He's finally awake! (*He pulls out a piece of paper from his armpit, unfolds it like origami and then folds it back into a square, inserts it back into his armpit, blows the air as if bubbles were elevating towards the sky, takes the piece of paper out again, observes its length and width, smells it, tastes it, and inserts it back into his armpit.*)

ELIQUIS:

Well, tell us, Mr. German Turnip!

KOHLRABI:

Never mind, it's not that important

ABIGATRA:

Unbelievable—

ELIQUIS:

(*crossly*). Don't you start.

KOHLRABI:

(*persuasively*). Hold on to your goats. (*He stares straight at* NGỬ.) He seems the most interested. (*He sighs conflictingly.*) I wonder why?

ELIQUIS:

We are the most interested! (*Silence.*) Forget God.

ABIGATRA:

(*to* ELIQUIS). Unnecessary blasphemy, don't you think?

KOHLRABI:
> It's because of God that I care to open my mouth.

ELIQUIS:
> When did you start caring?

KOHLRABI:
> (*To* ELIQUIS *and* ABIGATRA). What I want to know is, is that goat Zeus or the Christian God?

ABIGATRA:
> It's impossible.

KOHLRABI:
> Anything is possible. If you go at it right.

ABIGATRA:
> Try asking if he had a wife named Hera.

KOHLRABI:
> What if he doesn't say anything.

ELIQUIS:
> Then he is a Christian God in disguise.

KOHLRABI:
> A bit arbitrary don't you think?

ABIGATRA:
> (*To* NGŮ). Is Hera your wife's name?
> (*No movement and no words from* NGŮ. *Nada. Zippo.*)

KOHLRABI:
> You can't expect God to be a cigarette lighter with a hinged lid. (*All three examine* NGŮ.)

ABIGATRA:
> Especially if we don't know if he has any lighter fluid left in him.

KOHLRABI:
> God has infinite fuel.

ABIGATRA:

I don't care about infinite lighter fluid, tell us about Tiresias though.

KOHLRABI:

If I crave a fag, would you—

ABIGATRA:

Would I use him to light it up for you? Certainly.

NGỦ *suppurates.*

ELIQUIS:

He's discharging!

KOHLRABI:

Is it lighter fluid? (ELIQUIS *moves closer to* NGỦ *to smell him.*) It's a pity if it is not. (ELIQUIS *pauses.*) So, is it or isn't it? (ELIQUIS *moves away from* NGỦ.)

ABIGATRA:

Here. I'll smell him.

ABIGATRA *approaches the goat, sniffs him, and resumes her original position.*

KOHLRABI:

So, what is it?

ELIQUIS:

You tell us about Tiresias and we—

KOHLRABI:

You rascals. I'll smell him myself. (*He walks up to the goat, but* ELIQUIS *winks at* ABIGATRA *and then she grabs* KOHLRABI *by one arm and* ABIGATRA *pulls him back by the other arm and they prevent him from approaching the goat.*)

ABIGATRA:

Tell us. (KOHLRABI *kicks the air with one of his legs*

indignantly.) Tell us, Mr. German Turnip.

KOHLRABI:

You can't treat me this way.

ELIQUIS:

Why won't you?

ABIGATRA:

(*gently*). Don't force us to punish you. (*Silence.*) Unnecessarily.

KOHLRABI:

I don't care about its odor. Let me go.

ELIQUIS:

Not until you give in to our command.

KOHLRABI:

Life has been so cruel to me.

(KOHLRABI *begins to weep*).

ABIGATRA:

(*To* ELIQUIS.) Is he weeping?

ELIQUIS:

I don't know.

KOHLRABI:

(*With astonishing vigor*). Of course I am!

ABIGATRA:

Tell us, please.

KOHLRABI:

Let go of my arms and I will . . . (ELIQUIS *and* ABIGATRA *stare at each other, silently consulting each other, and finally they release him. He pretends to wipe a few fake tears*)… God doesn't excrete any lighter fluid. If he does, I would have smelled him from here. (*He broadens his shoulders widely and pompously.*) No, no, no. God does not have infinite resources.

ABIGATRA:

Are you a servant of time?

ELIQUIS:

He's no servant.

KOHLRABI:

You sure you want to know? There are consequences to knowing these things.

ELIQUIS:

We hold—

ABIGATRA:

Ourselves completely accountable.

KOHLRABI:

Alright then. Like I didn't warn you. Tiresias, my great great whatever grandfather, was reprimanded by Hera for a mistake he made, and she transformed him into a woman.

ABIGATRA:

My god.

ELIQUIS:

What was his mistake?

KOHLRABI:

In a time, when same-sex relationships were not forbidden, but considered distasteful. By the gods. He caught Hera having sex with a woman.

ABIGATRA:

She's bisexual?

ELIQUIS:

That's terrible.

ABIGATRA:
>I had no idea. She seemed so straight. Straighter than straight. I could see Zeus being queerish in a bear den sort of way, but Hera? Really?

ELIQUIS:
>She's so into herself.

ABIGATRA:
>Maybe that's why she has Sapphic tendencies.

KOHLRABI:
>So she visually impaired him.

ELIQUIS:
>Well, being blind makes him an unreliable witness.

KOHLRABI:
>Tiresias's mother, my great so great grandmother, Chariclo, felt sorrow for her sightless son and begged Zeus to undo the curse. Zeus couldn't undo the curse without receiving great wrath from his wife, so he gave Tiresias a different kind of sight: blind, but the ability to see the future. Anyhow, you'd think that would be the end of Tiresias's troubles.

ABIGATRA:
>What else happened to him?

ELIQUIS:
>Hera cut out his tongue because he knew too much?

KOHLRABI:
>Here is the worst of it. Hera and Zeus were having marital problems. After the Semele dilemma, they agreed to try polyamory. For the safety of most mortals. They often bickered over the conditions and terms of it.

They sort of agreed that they won't fuck each other's erotic lovers for the sake of sanity and septic cleanliness.

ELIQUIS:

So what's the problem?

ABIGATRA:

And, how was Tiresias involved?

KOHLRABI:

(*mischievously*). Ladies, calm down now. (*He tries to scratch his armpits, but the piece of paper gets in the way.*) Anyway. Although Hera and Zeus both agreed to the polyamorous bind, Hera felt that Zeus, being the womanizer that he was, seemed to get the better end of the deal. She thought it would be more satisfying if she had an advantage over Zeus. For some perverse reasons, she felt less insecure about her womanhood, her fuckhood, if she did something about it. And, having blinded Tiresias once, she felt she had no choice but to turn Tiresias into a woman.

ABIGATRA:

Better than a soap opera.

ELIQUIS:

So did Zeus fuck Tiresias?

KOHLRABI:

Well, there was a loophole in the art of cursing. A double curse removed the original curse. And, although Tiresias had become a woman, she was not blind. Zeus couldn't fuck her. He would know that Tiresias was once a "he," part of Hera's trick and wit—giving Zeus what he lusts but was appalled to have, and Zeus being as transphobic as he was, preferred women, or mortals who were authentically women. Not women who pretended that they are "women."

ABIGATRA:

Hera had Tiresias to herself.

ELIQUIS:

They became lovers, didn't they?

ABIGATRA:

For seven years?

KOHLRABI:

How do you know?

ABIGATRA:

From experience.

ELIQUIS:

(*quivering with amazement*). You are, you are—

KOHLRABI:

This can't be.

ELIQUIS:

Noooooooooooooo!

KOHLRABI:

I think I am going to burst.

ELIQUIS:

Impossible!

ABIGATRA:

I foresaw this many galaxies ago, my exponential grandson. The way time bends, light bends, space bends…

KOHLRABI:

Exponential grandmother!

(*They embrace, hug, kiss, touch, glance at each other up and down in astonishment.* ELIQUIS *watches on at their incomprehensible reunion.*)

ABIGATRA:

(*beaming with tears*). Oh, how, how I begged you to tell the story.

KOHLRABI:

(*overjoyed*). You were so adamant!

ELIQUIS:

Oh, why wasn't I cursed with some fancy supernatural ability?

KOHLRABI:

(*His head turns towards* NGỦ). Is that goat, Zeus?

ABIGATRA:

No.

KOHLRABI:

How unfortunate. (*Looking around*). Why are we here?

ABIGATRA:

I brought you here. (*To* ELIQUIS *and* NGỦ) Them too.

KOHLRABI:

Why?

ABIGATRA:

It has been seven years, and I have traveled far and wide. Through all kinds of universes. I have lived so many lives. It doesn't seem like it, the way my existence bends space and time, but I have arrived here to return to the skin I live in. Once again.

KOHLRABI:

We will help you. We will!

WAITING FOR GOD

(*The stage darkens. Exit* KOHLRABI, *Exit* ELIQUIS, *Exit* ABIGATRA. *Light faded. Light out.*)

Vi Khi Nao's work includes poetry, fiction, film, play, and cross-genre collaboration. She is the author of the novel, *Fish in Exile*, the story collection, *A Brief Alphabet of Torture* (winner of the 2016 FC2's Ronald Sukenick Innovative Fiction Prize) and of five poetry collections: *Bell Curve Is A Pregnant Straight Line, Human Tetris, Sheep Machine, Umbilical Hospital,* and *The Old Philosopher* (winner of the 2014 Nightboat Prize). She was the fall 2019 fellow at the Black Mountain Institute. https://www.vikhinao.com

www.ingramcontent.com/pod-product-compliance
Lightning Source LLC
Chambersburg PA
CBHW021449070526
44577CB00002B/329